Killing The Rainbow
Violence Against LGBT

by RJ Parker

Killing The Rainbow
Violence Against LGBT

by RJ Parker

ISBN-13: 978-1987902105
ISBN-10: 1987902106

Copyright and Published (08.2016)
by *RJ Parker Publishing, Inc.*

Published in Canada

Copyrights

Table of Contents

Introduction

The lesbian gay bisexual and transgender (LGBT) community has faced violence, hate and persecution for a very long time. Gay men, lesbians, transgender or intersex people have been targeted in a number of violent crime cases over the years. Usually, the perpetrators of these hate crimes are fanatics or homophobes who believe that these people defy the heteronormative gender roles and, hence, are not fit to be part of the society.

Various acts of violence involving assault, torture, harassment, and sometimes even murder, have been carried out against members of the LGBT community. Other than that, homosexuals, bisexuals and transgender people have also faced constant discrimination in their everyday lives on the basis of their sexual orientation. This discrimination against members of the LGBT community stems from religious beliefs, political views, bias or even internal fear.

The hatred and discrimination which these people experienced over the last fifty years or so, led to many of them losing their lives as a result of physical abuse. Even today, when the situation has improved and homosexuality is accepted in almost all Western countries, members of the LGBT community still get targeted in hate crimes.

According to recent statistics,[1] the Federal Bureau of Investigation (FBI) revealed that more than 20 percent of the hate crimes that were reported to the authorities were committed on the basis of perceived sexual orientation.

In order to explore this in more detail, let's go back to the beginning.

What exactly is a hate crime?

Basically, a hate crime is any act involving abuse, discriminatory behavior and prejudice against people because of their identity, religion, caste, creed or color. Victims are selected on the basis of their beliefs or orientation, and sometimes even due to general perception.

For decades, LGBT people have been victimized in numerous hate crimes all across the globe. While the situation may have changed in the Western world, there are still some countries in the Middle East and Africa where homosexual activities are punishable by death.

In countries where the Islamic ideology is dominant, homosexuality in particular is not acceptable. This is why they categorize any acts involving such activities as criminal and deserving of maximum punishment. Sometimes, however, the state may just fine or imprison the 'implicated' persons. Homosexuality, often considered as sodomy, remains the most prominent offense which is criminalized in a number of Asian and African countries.

Despite several campaigns and movements from the international human rights committees condemning these laws which make consensual homosexual acts a crime, there has been little progress in these regions.

Over time, the Western world has become more accepting and tolerant of the LGBT community. Many European countries classify abuse and violence against these people as hate crimes, while there are several bills in motion which aim to protect them from sexual-based discrimination. From 1990, the authorities in the United States have been avidly collecting data and observing figures on hate crimes, particularly gender-motivated ones.

Since the *Hate Crimes Statistics Act* was passed in 1989,[2] it has become easier for the legal bodies to follow such criminal activities and bring them to the attention of the government.

It has already been established that the LGBT persons faced persecution and violence from the very beginning. This may sound slightly vague, which is why it is important to look at it from a historical perspective in order to get a better idea of this matter.

History

A number of experts and analysts, who report on this subject, trace the history of violence against LGBT members to the Medieval and Middle Ages. Some say that it goes back even longer; however, due to the lack of substantial records, no concrete evidence can be presented. Still, certain historians and experts have pointed out the date when the first penalty was carried out against people guilty of 'sodomy'.

Historically, the state itself used to punish the individuals allegedly involved in homosexual acts or sodomy. In those days, the sexual offenses were limited to homosexuality and rape. The penalty for same-sex relations was death or public execution. Earlier depictions from the Middle Ages show that the people found guilty of such acts were responsible for unleashing the wrath of the gods and, hence, subject to the highest form of punishment.

Early Records

According to some sources, the earliest records of laws against homosexuality can be found in the Hebrew writings. There was a specific law in their commandments which prohibited sexual intercourse between men. Another one found in the Middle Assyrian Law Codes is just as old as the Hebrew law, but prescribes a more violent punishment for those found committing the act. [3]

This law states that if a man was found lying with another, they would 'prosecute and convict him' and then castrate him publicly. Experts have gone on to say that this particular law does not refer to homosexuality but, in fact, instigates action against homosexual rape.

Apart from these, there are other accounts which cite laws and penalties against homosexuality in the earliest of times. Historians found that in this era, there were mainly two criminal offenses which were punishable by death: one was treason and the other was immorality. Immoral acts have been translated as those involving prostitution, homosexuality and cowardice. Relationships between men were looked upon as weak and effeminate behavior, hence deeming homosexuality as a capital offense.

Middle Ages

Before the Roman Empire came under Christian rule, homosexuality was an offense punishable through fine or imprisonment. However, all the accounts and records from those times carry vague prescriptions of laws against homosexuality. The little that is deciphered indicates that men who willingly participated in same-sex acts may have been prosecuted but never punished by public executions.

Afterwards, when the Empire started implementing Christian laws, homosexuality became prohibited throughout and any activity was to be penalized heavily. The Christian Emperors soon declared same-sex relationships illegal and banned them. The rulers who followed these emperors took it one step further. They not only categorized homosexuality as illegal but also formulated a law that anyone found involved in such acts would be burned alive in front of the public.

Homosexuals were regarded as 'scapegoats' by religious advisors and higher officials. Any kind of wrongdoing or natural disaster was blamed on homosexuality, which is why the punishment for it became so severe.

Almost all of the regulations and laws that came through the fourth to fifteenth centuries in Europe banned homosexual relationships and prohibited practice.

The Middle Ages saw the City of Florence and Kingdom of France announce the death penalty for homosexuality as well. It has been noted that one of the very first hate crimes against a homosexual was carried out during this era. In 1365, fifteen-year-old Giovanni di Giovanni was found guilty of sodomy in Florence and, as per the law in the city, he was handed out a severe death sentence. Giovanni's thighs were burned and he was castrated as part of the punishment.

These violent acts continued throughout the ages, and homosexuality went on to remain a capital offense. Even during the beginning of the Renaissance, there were death penalties handed out to the guilty. Knight Richard von Hohenberg was found in a relationship with his young squire, and they were burnt alive together.

Jacques Chausson, a French writer, allegedly attempted to seduce a nobleman's son. He was found guilty and publicly executed. During this time, state prosecution of the homosexual, bisexual and transgender people was in full swing. Anyone perceived of being in a same-sex relationship or involved in any such activity was immediately given a death penalty.

The English also made homosexuality (termed sodomy) and acts of bestiality punishable by death in 1534.This law remained in place till 1861, after which it was replaced. There were no more public hangings and no further death sentences were given out against homosexuals after 1835.

Modern Age

This era brought with itself two major global events which would change the dynamics of the world order. World War I and World War II saw the biggest nations in the world embroiled in a quest for power against each other. As far as the persecution of the LGBT community goes, there was little development on that front. In the beginning, the situation remained more or less the same, with one exception. Homosexuality was no longer a capital offense in Europe as well as other Western regions.

The Nazi-ruled Germany targeted homosexuality as part of the cleaning movement, [4] with one man being executed by the right-wing rebels. Hitler's allies also frowned upon homosexuality and believed that these individuals had to be targeted for their sexual orientation. The Neo-Nazis used the German word for gay, Schwul, to demean others and equated homosexuality with weakness.

As time progressed, the circumstances became increasingly different. The LGBT community started to gain acceptance in the Western world, particularly Europe. There were campaigns and movements for the rights of the LGBT persons, with many notable personalities advocating this cause.

In the recent times, homosexuality is legal in almost every country across Europe and the North American region as well. However, this does not mean that the community does not face its fair share of challenges. Even in this day and age, incidents involving hate crimes against the LGBT persons are reported frequently. A lot of such crimes go unreported as well, which creates difficulty for the authorities and human rights committees.

The acceptance that the LGBT community has garnered from the Western world comes after a long and hard struggle. The gay rights campaigns and awareness regarding the oppression the community was facing every day started to spread after a few incidents made headlines across the globe. These incidents revolved around transgender people, gay men and women who lost their lives as a result of brutality and abuse they suffered at the hands of fanatics.

The social movements for gay rights actually began in the post Second World War era. However, the twentieth century had already set the groundwork for it. Slowly and gradually, people everywhere were becoming more conscious of the subject and homosexuality was no longer being regarded as an illness or a danger to society.

The Rise of the Gay Rights Movements

While gay rights did not officially become a reality until the mid-twentieth century, the seeds had already been planted long ago. The matter was a controversial one, which is why any movement that began to spring up was repressed in its early stages. It wasn't until the end of World War II that gay rights campaigners began to openly talk about equality and proactively formed liberation movements. [5]

Interestingly enough, gay rights awareness was not always subdued. In the early days, people wrote and argued on the subject but preferred to remain anonymous due to fear of punishment.

During the nineteenth and eighteenth centuries, Europe had strict laws against homosexuality, and cross-dressing was severely frowned upon. Experts have pointed out that while cross-dressing was prohibited, there were some exceptions. Certain male performers and theatre artists were constantly made to dress as women since female roles could not be played by actual female actors.

One of the earliest published works defending homosexuality was written by Thomas Cannon in 1749 and titled '*Ancient and Modern Pederasty Investigated and Exemplify'd*'. This work did not survive altogether, but historians managed to identify a humorous anthology which advocated homosexuality. The enthusiastic tone of the subject was apparent from the writing.

In 1785, social reformer Jeremy Bentham penned the first argument for reforming the homosexual law in England. At this time, the official punishment for homosexuality in these lands was a death penalty. Bentham was a follower of the utilitarian school of thought, and this was the basis of his argument which stated that the consequence of any action is reflected on the well-being of another.

He explicitly argued that homosexual behavior and tendencies were harmless and, hence, should not be regarded as a criminal offense. Bentham also went on to state that all the prejudiced and biased views against homosexuality stemmed from a rigid religious ideology, and there was no rational basis to any of the perpetrated hate.

The argument did not go public until 1978, and Bentham kept it quiet during his time as he feared that there would be a strong backlash.

This secular and humanist thought that had been the catalyst behind Bentham's argument prevailed through the French Revolution. In fact, experts say that when the new National Assembly in France came up with new laws and reforms, a group of gay advocates petitioned for their right of freedom and legitimacy. Jean Jacques Régis de Cambacérès, who worked upon the Napoleonic code, actually supported this petition and actively advocated it. His efforts were ultimately successful, as France became the first country to decriminalize homosexuality in 1791.

Soon other nations started following suit. In 1830, the Brazilian Empire established a new penal code within the region and decided to forgo the amendment criminalizing homosexuality. Three years later, an English writer, who preferred to remain anonymous, published a piece in favor of homosexuality. His writing was inspired by Captain Nicholas Nicholls and was purely in his defense. The Captain had been found guilty of homosexual relations and was handed out a death penalty in London.

A few years later, another writer from Switzerland, Heinrich Hoessli, had his writings on same-sex relations published. The first volume of his work was aptly titled '*Eros: The Male Love of the Greeks*'.

Despite all this, the society's attitude towards homosexuality remained fiercely negative and hostile. The Criminal Law Amendment Act in 1885 stated that any act of indecency between two men would be considered criminal and the people involved would be brought up on charges. This Act saw the conviction of successful playwright Oscar Wilde as he was sentenced for gross indecency towards other male members of the society. He spent two years in jail with hard labor.

In the 1870s, an advocacy movement for homosexuality began to make rounds. Aidan Buchanan, along with other notable figures, defended same-sex relations but kept all their identities hidden due to the sensitive nature of the matter. A secret society called the Order of Chaeronea was formed in Britain and counted these famous figures amongst its members. Even Oscar Wilde was believed to be recruited by this society.

The primary aim of the society was to campaign for the rights of homosexuals and ultimately get the state to legalize same-sex relations. The Order of Chaeronea was founded by one of the very first campaigners of gay rights, George Cecil Ives. He had been working tirelessly to end oppression and discrimination against homosexuals. It had become a personal 'Cause' for him.

Wilde met Ives at a club and was instantly attracted to his boyish charm. In fact, it has been claimed that the two even shared a brief, passionate relationship. Lord Alfred Douglas, Oscar Wilde's alleged lover, was also recruited by Ives for his cause, and he even introduced him to other poets in his circle.

Ives presented his cause in front of these notable Oxford writers and recruited a number of them for the campaign. Soon enough, the group was large enough for him to form the secret Order. This society, founded in 1897, became the very first platform for the launch of a gay rights movement in an era where it was absolutely forbidden. Members of the Order of Chaeronea included Samuel Elsworth Cottam, Charles Kains Jackson, John Gambril Nicholson and Montague Summers.

One of Ives's acquaintances, poet John Addington Symonds, was also an early promoter of homosexuality. A published piece of his writing, called '*A Problem in Greek Ethics*', became revolutionary later on and has been called a work of gay history. Even though medical writer C. G. Chaddock is usually credited for introducing the word 'homosexual' into the English language during 1892, it had already been used earlier by Symonds in his piece.

John Symonds was also responsible for translating a lot of classical poetry in accordance with homoerotic themes. Not only that, many of his own poems were also inspired by Greek images and literature.

His most notorious homoerotic poem, 'Eudiades', draws on this ancient language as well as imagery that captured his attention due to its controversial nature.

While the strictness of the Victorian society in England prohibited Symonds from talking about homosexuality in the open, his work spoke for him. All his published writings that were circulated amongst the average audience carried heavy undertones of same-sex love references. Experts have stated that his was the first work in English literature which actually cited direct sexual relations between two men. As Symonds grew old, his homosexuality became clear within the literary circles of that era.

Historians believe that John Addington Symonds's memoirs are amongst some of the earliest autobiographical records penned self-consciously by a homosexual writer.

Ives had recruited a number of renowned writers and socialists for his cause. Symonds was just the beginning. His friend Edward Carpenter was also a poet who started a campaign against the discrimination of homosexuals on the basis of their sexual orientation. Carpenter was believed to be greatly inspired by John Symonds and actually put his campaign into motion after Symonds's death. He also held the view that homosexuality was an inherent characteristic and opposed its criminalization strongly.

Edward Carpenter was one of the very few people who did not consider it as a sin and was expressively against this ideology. A book he wrote in 1908, '*The Intermediate Sex*', actually went on to become the foundation of the primary LGBT rights movements that started in the twentieth century. [6]

The social reformist inspired quite a few works regarding this subject. Carpenter's views that homosexuality should not be considered as a crime or a sin were reflected in a scientific study published in 1897. The book was written by an English sexologist named Havelock Ellis and carried the title, '*Sexual Inversion*'. At first, it was printed in German but was translated into the universal language after a year. [7] In this study, Ellis pointed out that homosexuality was not a disease or any scientific condition. He further went on to say that same-sex relations should be viewed as an important aspect of nature and not as a crime. His argument was against the restrictions imposed by societal norms on homosexuals, and it called for their freedom of practice. This book carried a lot of controversial matter which ultimately became the reason for its banning. One bookseller was even tried in court and charged for holding a copy of Ellis's work.

Twentieth Century

These early campaigners paved the way for what was about to take the world by storm.

While in their time, these notable figures were unable to do much about gay rights and legalization of homosexuality, they certainly set up the groundwork for future movements. Edward Carpenter, for example, went on to become a symbol of freedom and equality for all.

His work was used as the model for a number of socio-political movements. An early campaigner of LGBT rights, Carpenter inspired the formation called 'free love'. Not only that, his critique of traditional society structures also led feminist movements against the enslavement of women and patriarchal subjugation.

One of the followers of the free love philosophy included Russian feminist Emma Goldman, who also considered Carpenter's work as an inspiration. She openly defended same-sex relations and was against the repressive laws.

Perhaps a pioneer of the modern LGBT rights movements is writer and doctor, Magnus Hirschefeld. Most of the efforts to understand the psychology and human sexual behavior in the twentieth century have been made on his part. Both Magnus Hirschfeld and Sigmund Freud presented a lot of significant insight into the human mind. The former's work in particular was greatly beneficial to the cause of homosexuals.

His writings and published pieces were hugely sympathetic towards the LGBT community, and stated that this sexual orientation occurred naturally in humans. It was not a mental illness or a disease. His work stirred up quite the backlash from religious individuals.

During 1897, Hirschfeld formed the Scientific Humanitarian Committee and used its platform to publicly campaign against the law which made homosexuality illegal. The doctor dedicated most of his life to furthering the movement for LGBT rights and even founded the historic Institute for Sexual Science in Berlin. It became one of Europe's best libraries which archived literature on gay history and culture.

This institute conducted numerous researches on same-sex relations, interacted and provided counseling to homosexuals as well as transgender people, and advocated other sexual reforms as well. Previously considered taboo topics like contraception, sex education and women's rights were discussed on open forums, and awareness began to spread, largely as part of the institution's efforts in this area.

However, all this would prove to be futile as Nazi-ruled Germany saw to it that all of Hirschfeld's work was destroyed and both the institute and library demolished. All books in the archives were burnt with the exception of one Swiss journal that remained a part of the LGBT movement later on.

Other than the European region, LGBT awareness was on the rise all across the globe. While in the United States, there were very few movements for gay rights before the Second World War, the community members still enjoyed a relatively peaceful co-existence. The Harlem and Greenwich Village area was known for its flourishing gay life in the prewar times. According to some historians, a secret society called Society for Human Rights was formed in Chicago during 1924, which campaigned for gay rights. However, after a short time, it was repressed and subdued by authorities in charge.

Countries like Ukraine and the USSR also experienced a distinctive rise in activism for gay equality. [8] Hirschefeld's acquaintance, Anna Ruling, delivered a public speech on the subject at his request in 1904. In the speech, she stated that men, women and homosexuals were three separate genders and should be classified as such. Ruling also called for a united women alliance in them and gender equality campaigns.

Her speech at the time garnered little response, but it became etched into the minds for its social progressiveness. Subsequently, a number of women went on to join the movement for sexual reformation in 1910, when German courts tried to prohibit sex between two women. While Friedrich Radszuweit had literature and magazines published in Berlin, advocating the cause, Helene Stocker became the symbol of the feminist movement. Interestingly enough, Stocker was heterosexual and yet a prominent campaigner for liberation rights.

Aside from Germany, the USSR was also experiencing social progression. In 1922, it decriminalized homosexuality by amending the Criminal Code of the country. For a country that was still orthodox and economically behind others, this signified a huge step forward. The decriminalization of homosexuality was a part of a bigger movement which eventually saw the state grant equal rights of divorce, legalize abortion and promote women's rights.

When Stalin came to power, all these progressive measures were refuted and homosexuality was criminalized in the region again.

The post-World War II era was when things really turned around. The LGBT movement became one big wave which swept across the globe. It also led to the formation of various liberation campaigns, some of which are still working for gay rights and equality.

Homophile Movement

The movement sprang across a number of European countries, including Britain and France, and spread across Scandinavia as well as the United States. The members of the LGBT community from all over the world met during the war as nurses, soldiers and volunteers. They came to a unanimous decision that it was no longer in their best interest to keep this matter quiet.

Hence began the homophile movement[9] with groups of men and women campaigning for legalization in Denmark and the Netherlands. It continued towards other nations such as France, Sweden, Norway and the United States throughout the years that followed.

The term 'homophile' was used by these small groups to emphasize the importance of their cause. They preferred this to homosexual since it signified that love was valued over sex.

In the United States, the first public organization for homosexuals was formed and supported by Reed Erickson. It was called ONE, Inc. and soon became integral to the promotion of gay rights across the country. This was a major step in the fight for equality and recognition for the LGBT community. Before this, there had been the much smaller Mattachine Society which supported gay men as a minority and acknowledged their cultural significance.

However, the society founded by Chuck Rowland and Harry Hay in 1950 operated quietly and was not that mainstream.

ONE, Inc. [10] was followed by a couple of other similar organizations like Daughters of Bilitis, a lesbian network which published writings and promoted interactions between community members. These few organizations were some of the primary catalysts in the movement for LGBT equality and legitimacy. In no time, they found support of notable scholars and sociologists.

In 1951, a paper titled '*The Homosexual in America*' was published by Donald Webster Cory. It emphasized the idea that gay men were a part of the minority and, therefore, should be legitimized as a group. Within a few years, Dr. Evelyn Hooker made a groundbreaking revelation after historically winning a grant to study gay men in 1953. Her study was based out of the National Institute of Mental Health and allowed her to publish a paper on her observations.

Dr. Hooker presented the study and her findings in 1956, creating quite a furor amongst the general public. She stated that the men in her study were just like heterosexual males, as well-adjusted and, in fact, were even more settled.

All through the 1950s and 1960s, the homophile movement continued. However, experts argue that despite the leniency in laws and growing awareness, members of the LGBT community remained at risk of persecution and being charged with criminal offenses.

The number of organizations for gays and lesbians increased, with a dozen more operating across the country by 1969. Even after a national organization was formed, the media avoided giving any attention to the movement.

In 1965, the country saw its first ever gay march, which may have paved the way for the modern LGBT rights movement. This march was held in Philadelphia, directly across from the Independence Hall. It was soon followed by protests and riots demanding equality and end of discrimination based on sexual orientation.

The LGBT youth organization called Vanguard was founded by Adrian Ravarour in San Francisco. The group led a demonstration for equal rights in August 1966. On the heels of this protest followed the Compton riots, where a group of transgender prostitutes from the Tenderloin District gathered against the police. These individuals were victims of harassment at the hands of police officials, which is why they rioted in front of a popular cafeteria.

Britain was not far behind the United States when it came to activism. In 1957, the Wolfenden Report was presented and published across the country. Before the report, there had been widely publicized incidents where famous men had been convicted of homosexuality. A committee of scholars sat down together and agreed to publish the Wolfenden Report to dispel the rising tensions.

In this report, the committee had tried to break away from the traditional societal norms. It recommended that homosexual relations between two consenting males should not be looked upon as a criminal activity. Furthermore, this report went on to say that the main purpose of the law was to protect the injured and oppressed and to maintain order among the public. It had nothing to do with enforcing a particular way of life on some people or interfering in their private matters.

This actually went on to become the basis of the Sexual Offences Bill, which was introduced in 1967. It was backed by both the Labour MP and Home Secretary. The passing of the bill led to the decriminalization of sexual relations between two males above the age of 21. In England and Wales, homosexuals would no longer be persecuted if the sex was consensual and all such activities were carried out in private. The 1960s marked a significant turn of events in the LGBT movement. America, along with other countries of the world, was changing its attitude towards homosexuality. Gays, lesbians and transgender people were becoming active members of the society in most of the countries where the movement spread.

Gay Liberation

Homosexual and bisexual activism was already starting to gain prominence everywhere. Towards the late 1960s, it began to progress even further. Bisexual activist Robert A. Martin, also known to some as 'Donny the Punk,' started the Homophile League in 1966. It was a student organization formed within Columbia and New York Universities.

A year later, this organization was officially recognized by the Columbia University, making it the first educational institute within the United States to legitimize a group of gay students.

In the two or three years that followed, bisexual activism advanced rapidly. The Sexual Freedom League in San Francisco was openly advocating for equal rights on various forums. Marco Rila and Frank Esposito were its key activists. The cause was further facilitated by notable members of the community coming out as bisexuals. During one of the LGBT meetings at a mental health facility of San Francisco, Nurse Maggi Rubenstein declared that she was bisexual. This led to bisexuals being involved in the facility's regular programs for the very first time.

While this time was one of the biggest turning points in the gay rights movement, it also saw a rise in the cases of violence involving the members of LGBT community. Towards the beginning, the '60s had witnessed great social movements such as Women's Liberation, Black Power and anti-war campaigns. These contributed to the more radical and aggressive changes within LGBT rights activists, causing them to stir up opposition and fight back vigorously.

The Gay Liberation movement also marked the incident of the Stonewall Riots in 1969. These riots were the culmination of all the cases of discrimination against the LGBT community.

Stonewall Riots

These riots [11] involved a series of violent demonstrations by the LGBT persons against the authorities, in particular, police officials. They were held at Stonewall Inn, Greenwich Village, located in Manhattan, New York. Experts say that this event can be considered the backbone of the Gay Liberation Front and proved to be a major catalyst for the modern day LGBT equality campaign across the United States.

Basically, the gays, lesbians and transgender people had realized post-World War II that they deserved to be accepted as a part of the society. However, the anti-gay sentiment among the people was rooted deeply and little was done to change anything.

When the homophile movement went into full swing, members of the LGBT community began to highlight equality for all and provision of rights. Initially, this garnered quite a lot of interest from everywhere; however, by the late '60s, things were almost stagnant. Various social movements like African American Civil Rights, Equality for Women and Anti-

Vietnam War demonstrations were taking place throughout the country.

Ultimately, these social campaigns went on to become the inspiration behind the LGBT community's more aggressive approach to opposition. However, in the beginning, these movements were the reason behind the downslide of the gay rights campaign since it did not seem that significant any more.

The early homophile organizations in the U.S had already been working hard to raise awareness between the people and change their perceptions about the LGBT community. The aim was to put a stop to all injustice and discrimination that gays, bisexuals and transgender people had to face in their everyday lives.

Homophile organizations were already campaigning for educational equality and the right of employment. The general belief was that homosexuals should be able to enjoy the same privileges granted to heterosexuals.

Background

The United States was reeling from the aftermath of the war when this call for a drastic social change came in. It led the government and concerned authorities to actively work against these forces of change and oppose them. The State Department conducted a thorough investigation on the number of perceived homosexuals employed by the Army and services.

During a Senate meeting, Chairman Clyde R. Hoey was quick to point out a report which stated that people who 'engaged in acts of perversion' were generally less emotionally stable than those who didn't. [12]

This report went on to say that 'the government agencies unanimously agreed that these sex perverts' were a security risk in the government. Soon after, more than 400 people were axed from their government jobs, around 2,000 federal applications were rejected and almost 4,000 people were dismissed from military service for suspected homosexuality.

During the '50s and '60s, FBI and police departments kept a watch over all the homosexuals known to the authorities. Even the United States Post Office tracked all the addresses where any material on homosexual behavior was frequently mailed.

The local government and authorities led strict opposition against the LGBT community. Restaurants and bars that were partial to homosexuals began to shut down, with their regular customers being arrested and outed publicly. City governance started to 'sweep' neighborhoods and public places in order to get rid of the gays, transgender and bisexual people found there. Cross dressing was frowned upon, and those who indulged in wearing the opposite gender's clothes had to face severe repercussions.

Educational institutes like schools and universities also began to expel the teachers or instructors perceived as homosexuals. A huge number of gay men and women were humiliated in public, harassed, bullied, physically abused, charged for criminal behavior, and sometimes even sent to mental asylums. This discriminatory behavior prompted them to lead double lives and keep their sexual orientation private.

In the Diagnostic and Statistical Manual, it was reported that the American Psychiatric Association categorized homosexuality as a mental illness. [13] In 1962, there was a widespread study conducted specifically to prove that this disorder stemmed from an inherent fear of the opposite gender, mainly due to childhood trauma experienced by a particular individual. However, this study was countered by Dr. Hooker's analysis that homosexuals were just the same as heterosexuals and equally well-adjusted.

The observation came as a surprise for the medical community but made Dr. Hooker a champion amongst gay, bisexual and transgender people. Despite all this, homosexuality continued to be listed as a mental illness by the American Psychiatric Association until 1973.

Unrest

The organizations started as part of the homophile movement were already proactive in the fight for equal rights. While they were able to meet openly and socialize without fear of being persecuted, there was still some staunch opposition from the authorities. The Mattachine Society [14] was the first one to unify homosexuals and present them with a platform for assistance with any problems.

It faced many challenges initially which prompted the founders of the Society to change their strategy and work on a different agenda. During 1953, the Mattachine began to campaign for acceptance within society and equality. They wanted the general public to know that homosexuals were not that different from heterosexual people and, hence, deserved to be treated similarly.

The women-only lesbian support network, Daughters of Bilitis, also shifted their campaign and encouraged their members to become a part of society.

All the while, the government kept on trying to repress these campaigns and halt them in their tracks. When ONE, Inc. started gaining popularity among the public, they went on to publish a magazine which would be circulated widely. The United States Postal Service refused to mail the publication which boasted material on marriages between heterosexuals and homosexuals. Claims were made that the magazine was vulgar and too obscene to be mailed to anyone.

ONE, Inc. eventually decided to pursue the case and took the matter to court. In a historic ruling by the Supreme Court during 1958, the organization won the right to have the magazine circulated via the United States Postal Service.

Over the previous few years, there had been a drastic rise in the number of homophile organizations forming all over the country. The members of these organizations were becoming bolder and more open with each passing day. Army Officer, Frank Kameny, was dismissed from service on grounds of being a suspected homosexual. He initiated the Mattachine Society in Washington, D.C.

Kameny regularly wrote about the similarities between homosexuals and heterosexuals, claiming that there was no significant difference between the two. He often addressed people from mental facilities and programs in order to prevent them from believing that they were promoting abnormality.

In 1965, the ex-Army officer surprised leadership of the homophile organizations by leading a picket of government buildings, including the White House, in a protest against employment discrimination.

These pickets came as a shock to many gay members of the community as well. However, protests became the norm as the movement picked up pace in the late '60s and there were quite a few severe confrontations with the police.

Compton's Cafeteria Riot

As mentioned before, this riot was held by transgender prostitutes in front of Gene Compton's cafeteria[15] to protest harassment by the police officials. The gay community also involved people who did not conform to gender stereotypes at all. This included men who dressed as women and were effeminate, androgynous women and people who did not live according to their assigned gender at birth.

These people, classified as transvestites, soon became the most vocal representatives of the repressed sexual minority. However, they defied the image that was being portrayed by the homophile organizations that gay men and women were the same as heterosexuals. This meant that the campaign for equality and respect in society for the LGBT community stood to be affected by the non-conformity of the transvestites.

This is why both the Mattachine and Daughters of Bilitis claimed that while the struggle of these people was similar to their own, the ideology was totally different.

In 1966, however, the gay and transgender people jointly protested along with the transvestites to protest the police harassment. The drag queens, sex workers and hustlers from the neighborhood of San Francisco were sitting in Gene Compton's cafeteria when the police raided the restaurant to arrest the men dressed up as women.

It led to a riot which resulted in utensils being thrown at people, windows broken and glass shattered everywhere. The chaotic situation ensued even days later when the protesters returned to break the replaced glass in the windows.

A renowned professor later termed the riot incident as an 'act of discrimination' on the basis of sexual discrimination. The incident proved to be a catalyst for transgender activism in San Francisco. It also led to the events of the Stonewall riots in Manhattan.

Greenwich and Stonewall Inn

Greenwich Village in Manhattan, New York, was already known for its prosperous homosexual population in the region. Gay men and women had settled in the area after the World Wars and enjoyed a relatively good lifestyle. In the following years, this establishment of gays and lesbians helped in the development of a prominent subculture throughout the city. Due to prohibition and moral policing, many settlements were driven underground which in turn led to the popping up of small bars and drinking places in the district. The homosexual community could actually meet and interact freely without fear of being arrested and charged as the authorities were unable to keep track of all the people in the area.

The early 1960s were difficult times for the homosexuals in Greenwich Village. They could no longer engage with each other openly and were repressed by the authorities. The Mayor of New York was actively running a campaign to rid the city of gay bars and restaurants in order to improve its image. This was part of the preparations for the World Fair in 1964.

Local bodies in the city were revoking liquor licenses of public drinking places, and the police department was involved in an undercover sting to trap and arrest as many gay men as they could. The entrapment of homosexuals by the police officers usually was a result of an elaborate operation, which saw a police officer court the interest of a suspected homosexual. When the officer got a hint that the other man was interested in moving things forward, he would move in to arrest him.

Most of the times, these arrests occurred on whims. Sometimes, the officer would offer to buy the alleged homosexual man a drink and then proceed to charge him with solicitation. There were countless arrests throughout the city on baseless allegations. A story published in the New York Post revealed that a man in the gym locker room was arrested for asking another man (an undercover police officer) if he was feeling all right. The officer had been exhibiting suspicious behavior in the locker room and that prompted the other man to question him about his condition.

These cases created controversy which is why few lawyers and attorneys would take the responsibility of defending the victims.

Ultimately, the Mattachine Society managed to put an end to the entrapment operation in New York City. They persuaded the new Mayor to stop the harassment of gay people and were successful in their efforts to stop the campaign against homosexuals. The Society then tried its luck with the State Liquor Authority of New York, which was revoking liquor licenses of bars and restaurants for serving homosexuals.

The Liquor Authority proved to be a difficult challenge. While there were no laws which banned the serving of drinks to gay men and women, the courts had still provided the Authority discretion to revoke licenses if they deemed it necessary. The criteria was that any business partaking in disorderly or suspicious conduct would have its license revoked and be shut down eventually.

All this led to very few places remaining where gays and lesbians could interact with each other without the fear of being arrested and harassed by police officers. During 1966, the Mattachine Society even held a 'sip-in' at a bar called Julius to highlight the discrimination faced by the gay community members in Greenwich Village.

There were no bars in the district which were exclusively owned by homosexuals. All of the remaining ones which catered to the LGBT community were facilitated by factions of organized crime.

Stonewall Inn was a similar establishment, controlled by the Genovese crime family. Members of the Mafia had invested in the previously heterosexual nightclub and turned it into a happening gay bar. Police officers were paid off in an attempt to keep them away from the place and would collect envelopes filled with cash from the owners every week.

The Inn did not have a liquor license and otherwise appeared quite shabby. There was no running water facility in the bar, utensils were washed once in a dirty tub and reused immediately, and the bathrooms did not function properly. It even lacked fire exits and emergency doors.

Despite all this, gay men and women still flocked to the Inn. The bar did not facilitate prostitution, although drugs and cash were frequently exchanged here. It was the only bar in the area which allowed dancing openly. In fact, this happened to be one of its primary attractions. Stonewall Inn came to be known for its diverse range of customers including African Americans and Hispanics.

Sometimes transvestites and drag queens were also allowed to enter the bar. Soon enough, the bar became the 'It' place for gay men and women in the city. While most of the customers were male, lesbians could be seen coming in from time to time.

Towards the end of the '60s, police raids were becoming increasingly common in gay bars and restaurants. Just a week before the riots started, Stonewall Inn was among the bars raided by the authorities on account of suspicious conduct. Three of the clubs raided in Greenwich Village were forced to shut down.

Rioting

On June 28th, 1969, the police department sent four officers, along with two detectives dressed as civilians, to Stonewall Inn. They reached the bar and announced that it was being taken over. The employees and management were taken by surprise since they had received no prior information of this happening. [16]

It was the custom for the management and owners of a bar or a club to receive a tip-off before the actual raid took place. While rumors had been circulating among the employees that there was such a possibility, they did not believe that the information was accurate. The timing of the raid on Stonewall was not right since the police actually showed up at the doors much later than the usual time during other raids.

This led some of the employees to speculate that the Bureau of Alcohol, Tobacco, and Firearms may have ordered the raid.

However, historians have found information indicating that it was indeed the police department that raided the Inn on its own. It was believed that the Mafia owners of the bar were extorting their wealthy clients, mainly those who worked in the financial sector. The blackmailing resulted in more money for the bar management than actually selling drinks to the customers. This news somehow got to the police officers who became angry at not receiving a cut of the extorted money. When it became apparent that there were no kickbacks or profits for the police in this scheme, the officers concerned decided to shut the bar down.

Four police officers, two men and two women, entered the bar dressed in plainclothes. The squad waited outside for their signal. Once the assessment inside was complete, the police officers called for backup via the pay phone in the bar. Immediately everyone was alerted and the lights were turned on. Approximately two hundred customers were present in the bar at the time of the raid and were locked in securely as the police barred all the doors and windows.

The customers in the bar reflected on the incident later and remembered how terrifying the entire experience was.

They recounted that the police divided them up in two lines and asked for identification. This was when things took an ugly turn. The drag queens and men dressed as women refused to co-operate with the police officers. There were complaints from some of the lesbians that the police officers were touching them inappropriately.

Actual trouble began when a delay occurred in the vehicles coming in to transport the alcohol seized. The customers who were let go by the police did not vacate the area as quickly as expected, and most of them remained on the premises to watch the scene. This attracted other people as well, and in no time around a hundred and fifty people had gathered around the Inn.

When the patrol wagons arrived, the police began to load the owners of the bar in. This prompted a few cheers from the crowd. However, when the patrons started being treated roughly, the tension began to escalate.

A woman repeatedly fought off the police officers when they tried to get her in the wagon. As she was being forced away, she instigated the bystanders to do something about it. Violence broke out. The crowd turned into a mob and started to wreak havoc around the premises, getting into a scuffle with the police. When the police tried to restrain the people, it further incited them. The angry group toppled over police cars, slashed tires and threw anything that they could find at the officers. A quick realization by one of the detectives resulted in some of the officers leaving the commotion with the police cars.

The Police Administration told the officers to go back to the Inn with more backup. Things started to turn even worse. The police officers on scene who were greatly outnumbered barricaded themselves. They managed to handcuff some people back in the bar in an effort to contain the situation.

People who were in the vicinity described the events that transpired that day and the following one as surreal. Nobody could believe what had happened. While the Tactical Police Force arrived to rescue their fellow officers, it became clear that they had been defeated by the angry mob. Never before had the police been so humiliated publicly.

The riots continued on into the following day as hundreds of people gathered around the area to protest against inequality and discrimination.

Aftermath

Realization had dawned upon the LGBT community that these events had changed everything. It was a new beginning to something good. Members called meetings and discussed the need for a Liberation Front, and the need to commemorate the day in history. The community now knew that they needed to work as one cohesive unit in order to achieve success in their endeavors.

Exactly one year later, in 1970, the first ever gay pride march took place simultaneously across Los Angeles, New York, Chicago and San Francisco. This was to celebrate the historic day of the 'Stonewall Riots.'

Immediately after the Stonewall Riots, two major gay activist organizations were formed. One was the Gay Liberation Front and the other was called Gay Activist Alliance. [17]

Publications openly talking about the similarities between homosexuals and heterosexuals became available everywhere. The Liberation moved forward with confrontational strategies, hence using the word 'gay' to describe themselves. It was taken as the opposite of straight and defied the acceptable term of normal sexual behavior.

Gay pride became a staple component of the movement. Notable figures and scholars supported the movement for Liberation. Soon enough, things began to progress rapidly. Countries began to accept homosexuals in the government jobs and services. Quite a few elected members of the political parties in Britain and America came out as homosexuals and went on to continue their jobs.

In the twenty-first century, gay liberation has actually witnessed a new era. While it is accepted widely and legitimized in Europe and America, there are still some places where there is opposition.

Opposition of Gay Rights and Equality

The LGBT community's struggle for equal rights is far from over. Hate crimes committed against homosexual, bisexual and transgender people still continue, and homophobia remains rooted within deeply. Religious factions view homosexuality as a sin and repeatedly speak against this behavior in congregations and gathering.

Sometimes, these religious speakers have sparked violence against members of the LGBT community as well. There have been many incidents over time where men and women have been assaulted and left gravely injured by a group of religious fanatics.

It is a known fact that Islamic countries have strict laws against homosexuality, and it is an offense deserving of the maximum punishment. However, this doesn't mean that members of the LGBT community remain free of harassment in other countries. Even in places where homosexuality is legal, many people have faced opposition and even abuse because of their sexual orientation.

According to a report in Brazil, published by one of the oldest gay rights activist fora, the cases of violence against LGBT persons prevail throughout the country. In a thirty-year period, almost 4,000 cases of murder were reported which involved gay men, women and transgender people. [18] Brazil is not the only country with violent crimes being committed against the LGBT community.

The FBI reported that the number of homicides concerning gay men and women has gone higher during the last ten years or so. One of the biggest reasons for this is homophobia.

In European countries, and America as well, these acts are classified as hate crimes. Usually, cases of verbal abuse and bullying also come forward where the victim is taunted for their behavior and isolated on the basis of their orientation.

Experts have noticed that the crimes involving physical abuse against LGBT persons are more brutal than the others. This pertains mostly to gay men, where cases have involved more multiple stabbing, rape and burning. Psychologists have pointed out that there is a display of intense rage in isolated cases of violence against homosexual men. The reason for this remains disputed. Some call it homophobia; others say it is one's own identity crisis that can sometimes lead to exhibition of extreme violent behavior.

Brutality and aggression in these incidents have shocked even the higher authorities. A number of cases have victims badly beaten, burnt, cut and tortured. A particular incident in the United States made headlines across the world due to its brutal nature. On March 14, 2007, 25-year-old Ryan Keith Skipper was found dead in Wahneta, Florida. [19] The police found his body dumped on an empty road, riddled with stab wounds.

His throat had been slit and the body thrown out on the street which was just two miles from his home. The alleged perpetrators of the crime were arrested and charged with robbery and murder. According to some reports, Skipper's killers had driven around in his car which was soaked with blood and bragged about committing the murder. Their contempt for the young man stemmed from their hatred against homosexuals. One of the men from the Sheriff's department later revealed that Keith was targeted because he was 'a faggot'.

This was not the only case. There were other incidents similar to this along with many more that went unreported. In Canada, a survey was conducted in 2008 which revealed that around ten percent of the hate crimes in the country victimize people because of their sexual orientation.

While most of the countries have moved in to formulate resolutions against hate crimes and impose legislation, work still remains to be done in this area. A number of gay activists have expressed their dissatisfaction with the system over time and believe that the perpetrators of such hate crimes are not properly punished.

Gay Pride Attacks

LGBT gay pride attacks garner the most attention from the media because of their public nature. Sometimes, the police provide protection to the marchers, while at other times it may not do anything to dispel the attackers. There have been quite a few incidents when police officers have taken little or no action to ease tensions in times of a disruption.

Most countries allow the peaceful march during gay pride; however, there are a few which try to ban and put a stop to these parades. This has led to the occurrence of some unfortunate incidents over the years where chaos has ensued and people have been injured.

Opposition against gay rights equality prevails and, despite all the social progress, some factions of society still look down upon members of the LGBT community. Bullying in high schools and disparity in certain institutions has resulted in a lot of unpleasant incidents through the years. Young boys and girls have been driven to the point where they attempt suicide or run away from home. Acceptance is something that eludes these people in some places as yet. [20]

Despite homosexuality being taken off the list of mental disorders by the American Psychiatric Association in 1973, there are still some orthodox communities who believe that homosexuality is an illness which can be cured. In countries such as Africa, it is looked upon as witchcraft and a curse, leading people to try and lift it off through herbal medicines and 'magic' potions.

Awareness about LGBT rights and equality is only prominent in the developed countries. The more underdeveloped regions of the world still regard homosexuality and such behavior as improper and disorderly.

There is still a long way to go as far as LGBT equality throughout the world is concerned. While it might look as if the seemingly impossible has been achieved, a lot of work and effort needs to be put in. Previously, nobody could even think that one day same-sex union would be allowed and made legal across the United States; now it is a reality.

Similarly, gay equality everywhere can become a dream come true as well. Certain regions in Asia have already begun to open up to the idea, while others may need additional time and convincing. Most of the countries in the Middle East and Asia boast Islam as the dominant religion and thus do not encourage or promote LGBT rights.

Islam does not allow for homosexuality at all, which means that in Islamic regions, it still remains banned. In fact, Iran made headlines a few years back when it hanged two boys charged with engaging in homosexual behavior.

Noteworthy Advocates

Over the years, a number of celebrities and high profile figures have openly supported gay equality. In fact, certain celebrities have come out as being gay or lesbian publicly. While in previous times, even notable figures of society refrained from saying anything on the subject due to its controversial nature, in this day and age, it is quite different.

People boldly speak for LGBT equality and against hate crimes being committed against them. Around a decade ago, the suicide of a young boy brought a lot of notable personalities out in favor of the LGBT rights and acceptance. Numerous anti-bullying campaigns are being run and endorsed by politicians, actors and business figures.

Not only that, popular singers and actors are also regularly seen marching in gay prides regardless of sexual orientation.

A famous quote by Hollywood actor George Clooney on gay rights captured the attention of the media.

He said, *"At some point in our lifetime, gay marriage won't be an issue, and everyone who stood against this civil right will look as outdated as George Wallace standing on the school steps keeping James Hood from entering the University of Alabama because he was black".*

UN Goodwill Ambassador and actress Angelina Jolie also went on record to say that she would not marry her partner until everyone in the country had an equal right to get married.

This only goes to show how the times have changed and everybody has managed to adapt with them. Hollywood celebrities are not the only ones who have supported gay rights; politicians, business leaders and others have also spoken in their favor.

Opposition for gay rights may be staunch, but so is the support. Change is evident and will come in time.

In the words of Ellen J. Barrier:

"Change comes, when every person is adequately benefited. We keep hearing about 'change.' Change will never come to all of society. Change can only come when the market system adequately provides all of the needs for all people. Millions are

living in poverty in the United States and, throughout the world, due to 'change' passing them by, they are struggling. Among them are high unemployment, the mentally challenged, poor education, many of them are homeless and hungry, sick and tired; such individuals look for ways to move beyond their prison walls that hold them back from moving forward. Through the corridors of their prison, they observe the wealthy getting wealthier. They see the market system passing them at a fast rate of speed. Hope has long left the majority of them. There is a price that must be paid for the sins of those who have built these prisons."

The world will see LGBT rights and equality become a reality. As of now, the struggle continues and hate crimes against the community remain a constant. The last twenty years or so have been particularly important in highlighting the difficult challenges that members of the community have faced. Several people have lost their lives and suffered from torturous abuse. Looking back at some of these crimes, it can be said that these incidents have not been setbacks in the struggle. In fact, they have actually spurred it forwards and contributed to furthering the cause. Gay rights activists repeatedly cite the violence incurred upon the members of the community and argue that steps must be taken to curb it and prevent such incidents.

LGBT Hate Crime Victims: 1970s to 1980s

The period following Renaissance, brought about some major changes in the general perception regarding LGBT persons. As mentioned before, the concept of homosexuality and same-sex relationships was not perpetuated in the early ages. Those who were found guilty of engaging in homosexual acts or raised suspicion were punished severely. In fact, until the mid-seventeenth century, the accused were handed out death penalties and executed publicly. [21]

The situation began to change when a few nations removed capital punishment for homosexuality and no longer hanged the guilty. With the progress of time, the LGBT community started to fight oppression and raise their voice against the gross injustice imposed on their members. In the post-World War II era, gay, lesbian and transgender people formed united platforms and alliances to promote equality for all. During 1970, the world witnessed its first ever gay pride march in New York, formed along the lines of the liberation movement.

Hundreds of LGBT persons were gathered together to commemorate the anniversary of the Stonewall riots and promote their agenda of equal rights. This pride march was also the very first time where the 'Out, Loud and Proud' slogan was raised.

Since then, the journey of freedom and equal rights has come a long way. Every year, in June, the LGBT community holds its pride march where hundreds of people take to the streets and celebrate equality. It may seem like these are the best of times for the gays, lesbians and transgender people, especially when it comes to freedom and liberation. However, the reality is quite different.

While there is no doubt that the LGBT community members enjoy a much more open lifestyle and are considered equal citizens of society, the discrimination still prevails. Surprising as it may seem, recent facts and figures all point to the gross injustice and discriminatory behavior that LGBT persons have to face every day.

In fact, not only that, the number of hate crimes against gays, lesbians and transgender people hits a new high with each passing year. Many of the cases reviewed by authorities have been about homosexuals or transgenders being physically abused, badly hurt and sometimes even murdered.

After the hate crime bill was passed in 1990, the government commissioned the Federal Bureau of Investigation to collect information and data pertaining to hate crimes. This helped the authorities concerned to isolate those who were against the LGBT community members.

Close monitoring of these cases over the years led the FBI to determine that almost seventeen percent of the total hate crime acts were motivated by sexual orientation discrimination. It was further revealed that after racial and religious bias, gender-based prejudice was the third highest motivator of violence and attacks.

According to the Bureau's reports, the lesbians, gays and transgender people, or those perceived to be, are more likely to become victims of violence and attacks as compared to heterosexuals.

The FBI has been collecting data and monitoring statistics since 1991. Their records show that over 100,000 cases of hate crimes have been reported in the last two decades, out of which nearly two percent stem from gender identity bias. Analysts have stated that these numbers are primarily based on those cases which are reported to the authorities. This means that those incidents which are not reported to the authorities have no record whatsoever.

In the United States alone, there are a number of hate crimes acts against LGBT community members which are not pursued by the authorities. Sometimes, the victims themselves do not go to the police or officials due to fear of being 'outed', while on other occasions, the concerned authorities lack evidence to follow the case. Experts suggest that the under-reporting of hate crimes against LGBT is due to the improper protocol in place for responding to hate-based violence.

As the governing bodies work on establishing legislation and pass laws which allow the authorities to act against bias crimes pertaining to sexual orientation, the situation remains stagnant on this front. This means that until definitive action is taken, the LGBT community members will continue to face discrimination and fight homophobia.

It has actually been proven for a fact that the reason behind most hate crimes across the globe is the inherent homophobia that still remains deeply rooted among various factions of society. Generally, many people are of the opinion that hate-based violence against LGBT community members occurs due to religious beliefs and extremism. However, that is true for only a certain number of cases. Most of the time, gays, lesbians and transgenders have been victimized due to an aggressor's strong homophobic tendencies.

A more in-depth observation of the hate crime cases against LGBT community revealed that in almost every one of the incidents, the abuse and violence incurred upon the victim was much more severe than other criminal acts. For example, the perpetrator would physically abuse, torture, rape and critically wound the victim, sometimes even killing them. In a study conducted during 1994 and 1995, the Los Angeles Human Rights Commission [22] found that the average case of LGBT hate crime yielded a higher level of violence than racially or ethnically motivated hate crimes.

Furthermore, a survey on high school students led to the conclusion that the gay, lesbian and transgender students were subjected to a higher rate of sexual abuse and rape than the heterosexual student population.

Regardless of all the effort that the Western countries have put in to increase LGBT representation and legalize homosexuality, the gender-based hate crimes do not seem to decline. In fact, with each passing year, the FBI reports a rise in the acts of violence against gays, lesbians and transgender people.

The underlying homophobia within some 'closed off societies' remains strong to date, which is why hate crimes against LGBT persons have been persistent through the years.

Following the Stonewall incident, there was a spark of outrage among various conservative and religious communities across the country. It led to a significant rise in LGBT violence, where a number of victims were targeted as perceived homosexuals or transgenders, and subsequently assaulted with some being murdered.

During the 1970s, reported cases of LGBT violence investigated by the authorities, listed around fifty victims who were either physically abused or killed. In March 1970, a gay man by the name of Howard Elfland was cornered by Los Angeles police officers and beaten to death. He had been staying at the Dover hotel under a pseudonym J. McCann when he was targeted by the police. He was heard screaming, "Help me! My God, someone help me!" as the officers kicked him, did knee drops on his stomach, and stomped him to death.

Two years later, in June, 1973, a gay club was burned down by an arsonist. This bar was located in New Orleans and hosted frequent gatherings of the LGBT members. The fire claimed the lives of thirty-two people. It was the deadliest attack on a gay club prior to the June 2016 terrorist attack at the Pulse Night Club in Orlando, Florida.

Robert Hillsborough was another victim of the continuous streak of LGBT hate crimes. He was stabbed to death in June 1977, in San Francisco, by a violent fanatic who kept on shouting 'faggot' as he charged towards him. A year later, a group of homosexuals was assaulted by a gang of youngsters in an area of Central Park, New York. The perpetrators launched the attack on this area, known to host meetings of LGBT community members, and beat several people with baseball bats and wooden branches. These gangsters were later caught and confessed to attacking the victims on the basis of their sexual orientation.

The same year, 1978, also saw a high profile case of LGBT violence take place. San Francisco's openly gay city supervisor was assassinated by his political opponent within the City Hall. Harvey Milk was murdered by Dan White, along with the Mayor of San Francisco, George Moscone. This incident led to widespread outrage within the LGBT community and the sentence given to White, about seven years, instigated several protests.

In 1979, an anti-gay ad was run by the local newspaper in Key West. This ad was part of the anti-gay campaign prompted by a Baptist minister of the county. As a result, Tennessee Williams became the victim of an attack perpetrated by five young boys in the area. Fortunately, he was able to avoid serious injury and escaped in time to save his life. This year saw a series of hate crime acts against the LGBT community members. Almost six months after the Tennessee Williams incident, there was another similar episode of violence. Terry Knudsen was targeted by three men and beaten to death in Loring Park, Minneapolis. This was the second case of gender-based violence to occur during 1979.

On September 7, 1979, Loring Park, Minneapolis, Minnesota, became the scene of another LGBT hate crime. Robert Allen Taylor was brutally murdered by a man who later told reporters that 'he didn't like gays'. Barely a month had gone by when seventeen-year-old Steven Charles met a similar fate in New York. He was cornered by four men who beat him to death on account of suspected homosexual behavior. Charles's friend, Thomas Moore, was also gravely injured during the fight; however, he escaped to a nearby residential area where help was summoned. A few days later, the police rounded up a group of men and asked Moore to identify the aggressors. It was later revealed that the men responsible for killing Steven Charles were gangsters, Costabile (Gus) Farace, Robert DeLicio, David Spoto and Mark Granato. Gus Farace, the alleged leader of the group, pleaded guilty to manslaughter charges and was sentenced to a long term of imprisonment. After eight years in jail, Farace was released on parole in 1988.

The violence against LGBT members seemed to decline during the following decade. From 1980 to 1989, about five or six incidents of hate crimes were reported to the authorities and investigated. Even these few episodes of violence claimed the lives of three men and one woman. Charlie Howard was thrown into the Kenduskeag Stream in Bangor, Maine, for being 'flamboyant and gay'. The episode, which occurred in 1984, saw Howard drown after being pushed off the bridge.

Just two years earlier, Rick Hunter and John Hanson had been rushed to the emergency room in Hennepin County Hospital. They managed to escape death but were critically injured after being badly beaten up by the Minneapolis Police.

In 1988, Rebecca Wight was targeted for being a lesbian and engaging in homosexual acts during a hike with her partner. She was shot by a man named Stephen Roy Carr, who admitted that the couple had angered him. During the same year, the dual murder of John Lloyd Griffin and Johnny Lee Grimble made headlines across the country. Richard Lee Bednarski was found guilty of harassing and shooting the two gay men in Dallas, Texas. He received a sentence of thirty years, which caused quite a controversy since it had never happened before in history. Judge Jack Hampton, who had issued the sentence, went on record to say that his decision was based on the fact that Bednarski's victims were homosexuals. He clarified that if they had not been gay men 'scouring the streets for potential partners', this incident would have never occurred. His comments stirred a lot of higher officials and bureaucrats, and were subsequently censured. Hampton also lost his re-election bid in 1992.

Despite all these violent acts against LGBT persons, the alliances and pride movements sped ahead with full momentum. In October 1987, around half a million people gathered together in Washington D.C. [23] to participate in the march for lesbian and gay rights. This also resulted in the formation of more LGBT organizations such as LLEGÓ (National Latino Gay & Lesbian Organization) and the LGBT employee group at A T & T called LEAGUE. Just four months after this march, over a hundred gays, lesbian and transgender activists met in Manassas, near Washington. They decided to mark the anniversary of the march as a National Coming Out day.

In the years that followed, the LGBT hate crimes became even more severe in nature; however, they did not dampen the enthusiasm of the freedom fighters. As time progressed, more and more people joined this LGBT liberation crusade, regardless of their own sexual orientation. Their efforts culminated in the decision of the United States Supreme Court legalizing same-sex marriage across every state in the country. By doing so, it became the seventeenth country to entirely legalize homosexual unions.

Other nations have also taken similar steps and allowed same-sex marriages through constitutional amendment. While certain European countries may appear more progressive on this front, it does not mean that they have been successful in eliminating LGBT hate crimes. In the data provided by various human rights organizations, it has been reported that countries like Germany, Italy, France, Greece, Netherlands and Norway constantly witness cases of violence against gays, lesbians and bisexuals.

Although the number of casualties may be less, the episodes of assaults and damage are similar. Apart from this, there have also been numerous attempts of attacks on gay pride marches over time, sometimes leading to chaos and injury.

LGBT Hate Crime Victims: 1990s to 2000s

The '90s brought with them a new wave of violence against LGBT community members. There was a surge in reported incidents of abuse, rape and murder which involved gays, lesbians, bisexuals and transgender people. The numbers went increasingly high, with Brazilian gay rights NGO reporting that around 3,196 murders in Brazil, committed over the period of 1980 to 2009, were homophobic. [24]

Similarly, the Federal Bureau of Investigation posted worrying statistics from the last two decades where about 1,256 hate crimes against LGBT persons were reported in 2007 alone. This was a six percent increase from the previous year, when acts of gender-based violence hit an all-time high. According to the Bureau, there was a fifteen to sixteen percent rise in the LGBT hate crimes in 2006 compared to the year before. In the year 2008, approximately 17.6 percent of the hate crimes were gender identity based, targeting 1,617 victims of the LGBT community.

Not only that, the past few years have seen some of the worst cases of violence against lesbians, gays, bisexuals and transgenders, with the most recent being the Orlando shooting on 12 June, 2016.

The data that has come in during the 2000s signifies the need for urgent action. According to a report in 2004, almost fourteen percent of the hate crimes committed on the basis of sexual orientation were against gays and lesbians, while one percent of these targeted bisexuals. Out of the total documented cases of gender-based violence, two percent were against heterosexuals. Ten years later, another report by the Bureau recorded that there had been an increase of more than seven percent in LGBT hate crimes.

In 2014, the LGBT community members became victims of various violent episodes, sixty-one percent of which were attacks on gay men.

The FBI noted that the data in 2014 was similar to that of 2011, which also had a high number of LGBT hate crimes reported. Almost 1,572 violent acts were committed against gays, lesbians, bisexuals and transgender people, making up a percentage of 20.4 of the total documented hate crimes that year.

Various reports by human rights organizations and authorities have noted that all the hate crimes which are committed throughout the country are increasingly violent in nature, particularly those pertaining to sexuality and gender identity. It was discovered that the hate crimes carried out in the name of religion or ideology saw only one rape and murder, while there were six rapes and five murders attempted on the basis of perceived sexual orientation.

The cases of LGBT hate crimes during the 1990s also caught the attention of people across the globe. Several of these violent acts made headlines everywhere due to the brutality and aggressive nature of the crime. Most of the perpetrators of these crimes were tried in court and handed out life sentences, to be served until death.

In the '90s, eighteen cases of violence against LGBT community members were reported, which claimed the lives of twenty people. The concerned authorities pointed out that the scale of violence escalated in each case, with the victims being found brutally beaten, tortured, raped and abandoned in a demeaning state.

The first hate crime that was reported to the police in 1990 involved a gay war veteran, James Zappalorti. Investigating officials discovered that he had been stabbed several times and left to die on the beach. He had served in the U.S Army at the time of the Vietnam War and had spoken out in favor of homosexuality. A few months later, Julio Rivera of New York met the same fate. He was murdered in the city by two men on the basis of his sexual orientation. The perpetrators later admitted to beating him with a hammer and stabbing him to death with a knife, primarily because he had come out as gay.

In 1991, a banker from Houston, Paul Broussard, was attacked and murdered on the way home. He was cornered by ten fairly young men, who beat him up badly and were responsible for inflicting the fatal stab wound that claimed his life. Broussard had been with two other men, Richard Delaunay and Clay Anderson, when the attack was launched. Both of them were injured gravely; however, they survived.

The ten attackers were eventually rounded up and brought to justice. Their convictions included probation, hospital bills, fine and funeral payments for the deceased, while the one who had stabbed Broussard, Jon Buice, was handed out a sentence of forty-five years imprisonment.

A high-profile incident occurred on October 27, 1992. United States Navy Officer, Allen Schindler, was killed by his own crew mate in Japan, on account of being a homosexual. The case created quite a furor in the country, inciting numerous debates and protests by the LGBT community. It was revealed that Schindler had been stomped to death inside a public restroom. He had complained several times about the harassment on board that he repeatedly suffered at the hands of those with staunch anti-gay views.

This case led to the gays and lesbians of the community triggering a nationwide argument on the selection of homosexuals in military services. This debate continued for a long time and eventually resulted in the historic passing of the *'Don't Ask, Don't Tell'* bill. [25] (DADT) essentially *"restricts United States military personnel from efforts to discriminate or harass closeted homosexual or bisexual service members or applicants, while barring those who are openly gay, lesbian, or bisexual from military service."*

Another high profile case followed in 1993. Brandon Teena, a very young trans man, was raped and killed by his male friends after being outed as a transgender. His girlfriend's brother allegedly discovered his real identity and threatened him to move. Soon enough, Teena was evicted from his cousin's trailer and forced to move. On a trip to Nebraska, he encountered and befriended two men, John and Tom. Later on, Teena settled in Falls City and started living a new life away from his troubled past. However, his two male friends were soon able to discover the truth about his gender, and it led to them humiliating and ultimately killing Brandon Teena.

The events leading up to the death generated a great deal of publicity and interest throughout the country. Teena's murder caught the eye of a filmmaker who went on to make the critically acclaimed and controversial movie, *'Boys Don't Cry'*, based on the incident.

In March 1995, Scott Amedure, outed himself as gay during an episode of 'The Jenny Jones Show' on unveiling secret crushes. He revealed that he had been attracted to his old friend Jonathan Schmitz for a long time. The surprise revelation did not sit well with Schmitz, who went on to purchase a gun and kill Amedure. When Schmitz realized that his friend would not back down from his claim, he aimed the shotgun and fired at him. After Amedure was dead, his murderer went to the police and confessed to his crime.

At the end of the year, there was another LGBT hate crime reported against a man charged with killing a trans woman. Chanelle Pickett was a twenty-three-year-old African American woman who was found dead in William C. Palmer's house. Upon further investigation, it was discovered that Palmer had killed her after an alleged fight, during which she had revealed her identity. When he found out that Pickett was a transgender, he wanted her out of his home. Apparently, the argument took an ugly turn, forcing Palmer to fatally injure Pickett. However, later on, officials discovered that Palmer had met her at the Playland Café, which was known to be frequently visited by LGBT community members. The patrons of that place stated that Palmer was a regular at the café and his preference for transgenders also happened to be quite well known.

In December 1995, a lesbian couple was brutally victimized in Medford, Oregon. Robert Acremant murdered Roxanne Ellis and Michelle Abdill in cold blood. He later went on to say that his motive for murder was the sexual orientation of the two women. Acremont admitted to having 'no compassion' for homosexuals or bisexuals and was of the opinion that they should not exist. In what was a historic decision for the LGBT population across the globe, a court convicted Acremont in the murder of the lesbian couple and sentenced him to death by lethal injection. However, this did little to turn things around for the LGBT persons, who were still targeted and discriminated against on the basis of their sexual orientation.

In January 1996, a gay man and his partner were attacked in Texas. Fred Mangione was killed on the spot while Kenneth Stern, managed to survive. The attackers were discovered to be neo-Nazi brothers who decided to launch an attack on the gay couple because of their sexual orientation. Ronald Gauthier, one of the two brothers, was handed out a probation sentence for ten years.

During the same year, two other cases of LGBT hate crime violence came to the attention of the authorities concerned. A lesbian couple was targeted in Shenandoah National Park when they were camping. Julianne Williams and Lollie Winans, aged twenty-four and twenty-six respectively, had been following the Appalachian Trail along Virginia's Skyline Drive, when they were brutally murdered by an unknown assailant. Both women were discovered by the police, bound and gagged, with their throats slit. Even after an extensive investigation and area wide search, the perpetrator of the crime was not found. As of now, there have been no charges or convictions brought against anyone involved in the crime.

The second incident took place in August 1996 when Nick Moraida was robbed and murdered after a standoff. The thirty-four-year-old Latino man was openly gay and hence victimized on the basis of his sexual orientation. Richard Cartwright killed him following a robbery but was captured by the police and tried in court. He was the second aggressor of a heinous LGBT hate crime who was given a death penalty.

Perhaps one of the most significant LGBT hate crimes of that decade was the bombing of The Otherside Lounge in 1997. This lesbian night club was located in Atlanta and was targeted by a man named Eric Robert Rudolph, also known as the 'Olympic Park Bomber'. His several bombing attempts led to the subsequent destruction of the club. Fortunately, there were no serious casualties during the incident, with only five patrons of the bar being injured. For his actions, Rudolph was sentenced to five consecutive life terms. In a statement released after his conviction, he stated that homosexuality was abnormal and considered an 'aberrant lifestyle'.

The following year witnessed the LGBT hate crime which changed the entire community. It is still cited by all the major lesbian, gay and bisexual alliances, and activists have made it into an example for the future. On October 7, 1998, Matthew Shepard, a homosexual student from

Wyoming, was found critically wounded in Laramie. He had been severely beaten, tortured and tied to a nearby fence before being abandoned by the perpetrators of the crime. The police were called eighteen hours after the incident, after a cyclist spotted Shepard's still form attached to the fence. Due to the physical abuse incurred upon him, he had gone into a coma.

The authorities rushed him to the county hospital but to little avail. Shepard succumbed to his injuries and was pronounced dead a week later. Aaron James McKinney and Russell Henderson were arrested for torturing and murdering twenty-one-year-old Matthew Shepard. They are serving their life sentences as of this date.

From February 1999 to October 1999, four reported incidents of LGBT hate crimes made headlines. Thirty-nine-year-old Billy Jack Gaither was the first victim found murdered in Rockford, Alabama. Authorities discovered that the gay man had been brutally assaulted and beaten to death by his attackers. Charles Munroe Butler and Steve Mullins were later convicted of the crime. The court handed out life imprisonment sentences to both the men, without the possibility of parole.

On July 1, Gary Matson and Winfield Mowder became the victims of a hate crime at the hands of two supremacist brothers. The gay couple was targeted on account of their sexual orientation by Matthew Williams and Tyler Williams. Both Mowder and Matson were killed in the incident.

The brothers were arrested and tried for all their crimes including the murder of the gay couple in Redding, California. Tyler Williams was sentenced to two terms of imprisonment; he was to serve thirty-three years in prison for his part in the murders after completing a twenty-one-year sentence for bombing a synagogue and an abortion clinic. His brother, Matthew, went on to commit suicide while awaiting trial in 2003. According to a statement released by the investigating officials, Matthew Williams had killed the gay couple to express his fealty for the 'Creator' and by doing so he had just been obeying God.

The Williams brothers' former pastor was recorded as saying that they had been 'zealous' as far as faith was concerned but not known to follow it accordingly.

Just two months after this incident, the Steen Fenrich case garnered worldwide attention. He was the third victim of an LGBT hate crime that year. A native of Queens, New York, Fenrich was apparently murdered by his own stepfather, John D. Fenrich. His body wasn't discovered until a year later when the police found dismembered remains with Steen Fenrich's social security number written across the skull. The investigating officers also deciphered a derogatory phrase scrawled along with the number and went on to question his stepfather. During the interview with the police, John Fenrich fled from the scene and later committed suicide.

On October 15, 1999, Charles Bolden's body was discovered in Savannah, Georgia, and it was revealed that he had been shot to death. The attacker was not arrested till 2003, when the police finally caught up to him and charged him with murder. It was revealed that Charles E. Wilkins Jr., the perpetrator of the crime, harbored a strong anti-gay sentiment, which was why he murdered Bolden. Wilkins Jr. admitted to the killing and was also charged with two other homicides by the Savannah Police Department.

The 2000s brought along some major positives for the LGBT community. The Obama government signed into law the bill classifying gender-biased attacks as a federal offense. [26] Same-sex unions were legalized and America seemed to be on the path of modern enlightenment in its entirety. However, the FBI reports clouded over the progress of the whole movement.

According to the statistics, the years 2000 and 2009 witnessed the worst cases of LGBT hate crimes. The incidents of violence against gays, lesbians, bisexuals and transgenders hit an exceedingly high number, with over a thousand people being victimized each year.

Arthur Warren's murder was one of the first reported cases of LGBT hate crimes in 2000. Two teenage boys targeted him in a street and beat him to death, repeatedly punching and kicking him. One of the attackers, David Allen Parker, believed that Warren had been responsible for a rumor going around that they had engaged in a sexual act with each other.

The brutal murder in Grant Town, West Virginia, gained a lot of media attention and spurred gay rights debates across the country. Warren's murder was made to look like a hit-and-run accident by the perpetrators, who ran over his body with a car. However, the police were able to uncover the actual cause of death and caught the killers. David Allen Parker confessed to killing Warren and pleaded guilty. He was handed out a life sentence in prison with mercy, meaning that he could be paroled after fifteen years. The other attacker, Jared Wilson, was sentenced to serve twenty years.

Two months after this episode, Ronald Gay targeted a gay bar in Roanoke, Virginia. He entered the bar and opened fire inside. Six patrons were gravely injured, while forty-three-year-old Danny Overstreet lost his life after being directly hit by a bullet. According to a statement, Gay was angry over the new meaning of his name and ashamed that three of his sons had even changed the surname. He identified himself as a Christian soldier acting upon the Lord's orders to look for gay men or women and kill them. His testimony in court was further proof of the deep-rooted homophobia. In front of the injured victims and Danny Overstreet's family, Gay admitted to the murder and wished that 'he could have killed more of these people'.

In 2001 and 2002, six members of the LGBT community were targeted on the basis of their sexual orientation. Fred Martinez was a transgender student who was bludgeoned to death in Colorado. The brutal murder was carried out by Shaun Murphy, eighteen years of age, who was caught when he started bragging about attacking a homosexual, or a 'fag' as he was reported as saying.

Philip Walsted was another gay man who was murdered by a fanatic. He was beaten to death by a baseball bat, and David Higdon was charged for it. Further investigations revealed that Higdon's neo-Nazi views were responsible for spurring the act of violence. Initially, his plan had been to rob Walsted, but things escalated when he discovered that his victim was a homosexual. Higdon was sentenced for life, including additional penance for robbery.

Nizzah Morris, Rodney Velasquez, Gwen Araujo and Terraine Summers were the other victims of LGBT hate crimes. They all lost their lives after being subjected to physical abuse and torture. The only exception to these cases was the murder of Terraine Summers. She was a fifty-one-year-old LGBT rights activist who was shot and killed in her own front yard. The crime was included in the list of hate crimes against LGBT community, but the police did not show any interest in investigating the motives behind the murder.

In 2003, fifteen-year-old homosexual student Sakia Gunn was attacked for admitting that she was a lesbian. She was stabbed and fatally wounded by Richard McCullough. The attacker was charged with her murder but avoided a life sentence as he opted for a guilty plea. McCullough admitted to committing numerous other crimes including second degree murder. The court sentenced him to twenty years imprisonment.

Richard Philips, Brandi Coleman and Nireah Johnson were three other victims of heinous hate crimes against LGBT persons. In June 2003, Philips was attacked and killed in Kentucky. His murderer, Joseph Cottrell, was convicted on manslaughter charges and given a twenty-year prison sentence. Philips's body was discovered in a suitcase found in Rough River Lake.

Brandi Coleman and Nireah Johnson were shot and killed by Paul Moore. During a sexual encounter, Moore discovered that Johnson was a transgender. He murdered both the victims and later burned their bodies. Moore was convicted and handed out a sentence of 120 years' imprisonment.

The following years saw a series of violent crimes committed against LGBT members. In fact, some of them were so heinous and brutal that they were quite unfathomable. A three-year-old boy died in Tampa, Florida, due to severe brain injuries. His father repeatedly beat him up after he suspected that the boy would grow up to be gay. A homeless and hearing-impaired man in Alabama was targeted for his sexual orientation outside his trailer. His assailants stabbed, tortured and strangled him to death. The perpetrators did not stop there. After killing him, they burned his body and left the remains near his mobile home.

A number of young and old LGBT community members became targets of homophobia-induced LGBT hate crimes during 2008 and 2009. Victims were shot, beaten up, raped and abused severely. In November 2008, there was a case of arson involving an openly gay man called Melvin Whistlehunt. A group of arsonists completely destroyed his house in Newton, North Carolina, and sprayed homophobic graffiti on the back of the property.

Just a week later, a trans woman by the name of Lateisha Green was murdered in New York. Her attacker, Dwight DeLee targeted her because of perceived homosexuality. The case of this twenty-two-year-old's murder became the first one in New York to obtain a hate crime conviction within the state of New York. DeLee was prosecuted and charged with Green's murder. This was only the second time in the history of the nation that a perpetrator was prosecuted and convicted of a hate crime against a member of the LGBT community.

These are just a few of the gender-based hate crimes that managed to provoke a response from the authorities concerned. Despite strict action being proposed by the government against the perpetrators, violence continued.

If one is to observe all the different cases of LGBT crimes from 2010 to the current year, it would become increasingly clear that the gays, lesbians, bisexuals and transgender people still have a long fight ahead. The numerous cases reported include those of murder, assault, torture and forced sexual intercourse. Other than that, there is constant bullying and peer pressure imposed upon those who appear different and do not conform to the set gender roles of society.

There have been incidents where young boys and girls have committed suicide due to bullying at education institutions and workplaces. In 2009, an eleven-year-old boy from Massachusetts, Carl Joseph Hoover-Walker, was found hanging from an extension cord. His mother revealed that he had been regularly bullied at his school and jeered at for appearing effeminate and gay.

Global Hate Crimes

The United States is not the only country on this side where LGBT hate crimes regularly occur. Canada, Australia, Brazil, France, Ireland and Israel are some of the countries that have reported rising incidents of hate crimes against LGBT community members. The United Kingdom also saw a number of gays, lesbians and transgender people being targeted on the basis of their sexuality.

Craig Zee, an Australian, was attacked by four men in 2007. He had been holding his boyfriend's hand out on the street when the perpetrators cornered and beat him severely, fracturing his skull. Although he was able to recover, the LGBT community had suffered a huge setback in their fight to freedom.

In Canada, the openly gay or lesbian people were targeted at random and physically abused by their attackers. A few of them also lost their lives after succumbing to injuries later on.

Similarly, United Kingdom and other countries reported various hate crimes against LGBT persons which claimed their lives or left them in a vegetative state. There were quite a few victims who survived the attacks but either became paralyzed or paraplegics. Gay pride marches have also been targeted with participants being badly beaten after separating from the public. In Israel, Yishai Shlisel stabbed three gay pride marchers and was sent to jail for injuring them critically. However, with a stroke of luck, all of them survived the attack. The incident occurred in 2005.

Ten years later, when Shlisel was released from jail, he targeted another gay pride march and attacked six marchers. Five of them were only wounded while one was pronounced dead.

Homophobic fanatics do not only victimize the average person but also noted personalities. Popular celebrities who have come out as gay, lesbian or bisexual are also attacked either verbally or physically by the hate crime perpetrators. Poets, writers and TV presenters such as Mark O'Neill and Brendon Courtney reported physical assaults launched upon them by gay bashers and anti-LGBT groups.

The fear of becoming a hate crime victim runs strong within the LGBT community. Almost more than fifty percent of the community members have expressed serious concerns for their lives and termed the situation as extremely worrisome. The LGBT youth in particular have called for quick preventive measures due to the alarming rate of transgender and gay teen suicides. Experts determined that the most common cause for this was sexual suppression, bullying and rape.

Crimes That Transformed The LGBT Activism

Numerous cases of violence against LGBT community members have been reported over the years across the globe. While most of these incidents are known for the brutality and extreme violence incurred upon the victims, there are only a fraction which have managed to actually change the LGBT community for the better.

Gender-based violence has incited continuous debates calling for the law to take action and establish preventive measures, some of which have culminated in the actual passing of laws or resolutions by the governing bodies. Over the years, the LGBT hate crimes have prompted the gays, lesbians, transgender and bisexual alliances to speed up their efforts for equal rights and liberation. In the past two decades, their journey has actually come a long way from where it began. Homosexuality is legalized, and same-sex marriages are allowed in every state in the USA since 2015. [27]

However, the struggle has not been without ups and downs; in fact, to this date, it continues as the war against homophobic ideology gains momentum with each passing day.

The International Day against Homophobia and Transphobia is observed on May 17, and around 70 countries unite to observe the occasion. Noted scholars and personalities gather together to discuss ways of dealing with LGBT crimes and propose legislative laws into action. Almost 50 countries have reported a rise in the hate crimes against gays, lesbians, bisexual and transgenders since 2008. Recently, Chile spurred its efforts to encourage LGBT anti-discrimination laws after the horrific murder of Daniel Zamudio.

Openly gay, twenty-four-year-old Zamudio became a target of homophobic fanatics and was severely beaten. He was admitted to the hospital and succumbed to injuries there. The case shocked Chileans nationwide, with the lawyer for Zamudio's family, terming it as the 'worst case of brutality witnessed since the dictatorship days'. When the news spread across the South American region, comparisons were made with the Matthew Shepard case.

Many people pointed out the similarities between the two incidents.

Zamudio's is not an isolated case. There have been quite a few cases of extreme violence that have prompted immediate action.

As previously mentioned, Houston-based banker Paul Broussard was targeted by a group of young men on his way home. The incident was dubbed as *'Houston's Stonewall'* by news-reporting entities. On July 4, 1991, Broussard and his two friends were cornered by ten men near Heaven, a gay bar. The incident occurred within the Montrose district, which is known for its heavy LGBT population.

The men attacked Broussard and his two companions with knives, steel toed shoes and nail laden wooden planks. While his friend managed to escape and survive, the twenty-seven-year-old lost his life and yielded to injuries after a few hours. His death incited numerous protests by the LGBT community of Houston, where protesters thronged the streets of the Montrose district. Gay protests were held outside the home of the city's Mayor. At almost 2 a.m., Mayor Kathy Whitmire had to deal with a large group of people protesting against the assault and subsequent murder of Paul Broussard.

The affluent neighborhood of Woodlands was alive with the chants and slogans of the gay protesters demanding action against the perpetrators of the crime. A group called 'Queer Nation' took the entire district and went on to protest outside the homes of as many attackers as they could find. This movement turned out to be the largest civil disobedience campaign in the history of Houston.

A member of the Queer Nation, David Fowler, went on record to say that the people had endured enough gross injustice and were now fed up. They would not take this anymore.

City Council elected official Annise Parker admitted surprise at the high volume of people that had taken to the streets. She expressed concern about Houston's situation and called for collective remedial measures. In just fifteen days, the entire council candidates, even the ones who had previously voted against LGBT rights ordinances, agreed upon a resolution to get a hate crime bill on the legislative agenda.

The perpetrators of the crime were tried and sentenced. The coroner's report determined that the stab wound had ultimately killed Broussard, and when Jon Buice confessed to inflicting it, the judge handed out a 45-year imprisonment sentence to him. He remains in jail as of this date, with parole denied each time.

The Broussard death acted as a trigger for the hate crime protection acts in Texas. A decade after the incident, these preventive measures actually took off; however, they still do not cover the transgender people. The Montrose District formed a remembrance garden at the same place where Broussard's murder took place. In fact, last year, this garden was dedicated to LGBT hate crime victims and is considered as a symbol to promote peace and tolerance.

Since then, around thirty people have been killed in the same area on the basis of their sexuality. This includes, Aaron Scheerhoorn, who was murdered in 2010.

Hampton Roads Killer

Between 1987 and 1996, twelve gay or bisexual men were brutally murdered and left in the secluded area of Virginia known as the Hampton Roads. The victims were strangled to death before being dumped. The cause of death for most of these people was determined as strangulation; however, a few were too badly decomposed to render any concrete conclusion. [28]

All of the bodies found were discovered in a nude state, with one exception. Investigations revealed that the twelve victims had been last spotted at various gay bars in either Norfolk or Portsmouth.

The incidents ignited an outcry of outrage within the LGBT community, due to lack of action by the police department and concerning authorities. Executive Director of Virginians for Justice, Shirley Lesser, said in her statement that as long as the general public didn't come together and ask for it, there was little the police could do.

She also went on to say that police resources are dependent on public direction and until the non-gay-friendly community called for it, they had to sit back.

However, soon enough, the police was able to arrest Jackson Elton Manning after he was charged with the murder of Andrew Smith, the latest of the Hampton Roads victims. His body was discovered dumped in the same area after being strangled. The modus operandi of the killer caused the authorities to allege that Manning was indeed the serial killer responsible for all twelve deaths.

Further evidence showed that Manning had engaged in sexual acts with victims Andrew Smith and Reginald Joyner. Blood from both men was found on his bed. The authorities tried him in court and eventually sentenced him to life in prison. While he wasn't formally charged for the other eleven murders, the FBI seemed to believe that he was the criminal. They released documents later which suggested that Manning was the man behind all those killings.

After his arrest, the violence halted and no more people were harmed in that area. Certain profilers remained conflicted about his modus operandi long after the conviction, since he was an African American whose victims were racially diverse. Until then, it was widely believed that serial killers targeted the same concentrated group of people matching a particular type.

Matthew Shepard

Shepard's murder was the single most important turning point for the LGBT community during the '90s. It ultimately led to the 2009 passing of the hate crime bill, 'The Matthew Shepard and James Byrd, Jr. Hate Crimes Prevention Act'. [29] Apart from that, his murder inspired films, plays, books and several other materials on LGBT violence at that time.

It garnered attention from the entire world due to the nature of violence involved, bringing focus to hate crime legislation at both domestic and international levels.

Matthew Shepard was a local from Casper, Wyoming, who was pursuing a political science degree at the University of Wyoming. At twenty-one years of age, he had just completed his first year. He was loved by all and was known to be the person whom everyone could relate to. Later on, it was also revealed that Shepard was raped in Morocco, during a class trip to the country. This led to him experiencing bouts of depression and anxiety.

On October 6, 1998, Shepard happened to be at a local restaurant called the Fireside Lounge, located in Laramie, Wyoming, where he ran into Aaron McKinney and Russell Henderson. Both the boys decided to give Shepard a lift back home, but instead of driving there, they took him to an abandoned area. Once at this remote place, McKinney and Henderson proceeded to beat Shepard severely. They robbed him, tortured him and then left after tying the unconscious young man to a fence.

The perpetrators returned back to the lounge and got into a bar fight with two Hispanics. The brawl led to a police officer arriving on the scene who searched both of them. Soon enough, Shepard's credit card, shoes and bloodied gun were recovered from McKinney. When they realized that the situation might lead to trouble, they tried to convince their girlfriends to alibi for them.

Almost eighteen hours later, Matthew Shepard was discovered by a cyclist passing by the fence, who initially mistook him for a scarecrow. When the police arrived on scene, they found him alive but in a coma. He was rushed to the nearby hospital and remained on life support for the next several days. While in the hospital, it was discovered through routine blood work that Matthew was HIV positive.

On October 12, Matthew succumbed to his injuries.

The trial held for the offenders established that they had pretended to be gay in an attempt to lure Shepard out. They were both convicted on counts of robbery, aggravated assault, kidnapping and first degree murder.

After the death of Matthew Shepard, petitions were made for active legislation on hate crimes against LGBT members. After numerous changes and inductions into the amendment, the U.S Senate finally decided to vote on the bill as an extension of the federal hate crime legislature. The bill was introduced in the Assembly on April 28, 2009. It was finally adopted by the Congress after a heavy vote in favor of the resolution.

President Obama signed the Protection Act into law on October 28, 2009.

Matthew Shepard

Sakia Gunn

The fifteen-year-old student was just like other regular high school girls. She loved to play baseball, have fun with her friends and was studious as well. Sakia was known to be a lesbian within the community; however she did not like conforming to one particular gender. Hailing from Newark, she was a junior at the N.J. West Side High School.

On May 11, 2003, Sakia Gunn [30] was standing near a bus stop along with her friends, looking to head back home after visiting Chelsea Piers. This area was known for its frequent LGBT gatherings and was located along the Hudson River in New York.

The group of girls was approached by two men who propositioned them to come over to their car. Gunn and her friends refused, admitting that they were lesbians, hence not interested in their proposition.

Near the bus was a police booth; however, at that time of the night, it wasn't staffed. The girls were minutes away from home so they were not worried about getting back in the dark.

Things took a turn for the worse when one of the men, Richard McCullough, did not take the rejection lightly. He jumped out of his car and started to beat up one of the girls. Sakia, along with one of her friends tried to stop him, only to get choked and assaulted as well. But she kept up the retaliation by fighting back hard. The shakedown ended when McCullough removed a knife and stabbed her before running away from the scene.

Miss Gunn was pronounced DOA at the hospital.

Her friends formed a memorial site where she was killed, and almost three thousand LGBT members turned up to pay tribute to her memory. Gunn's death also mobilized the African American lesbian community, which led to the creation of the Newark Pride Alliance.

The police booth near the bus stop has been fully staffed from that day onward, as promised by the Mayor of Newark.

Modern Day Crimes

In the last three or four years, LGBT crimes have continued at a rapid pace all across the world. The Muslim countries are not the only states where these criminal acts have occurred. The African nations and Western countries have witnessed similar cases of hate crimes against LGBT community members and even their supporters.

Eric Lembembe, journalist who blogged about his pro-LGBT rights campaign, was found murdered in Cameroon. His body was discovered in his apartment where he was tortured to death. His hands and feet were broken and had multiple burn marks from an iron. The killer(s) were never caught. [31]

Eric Lembembe

Within the same year, a transvestite was killed in Brazil after he was riddled with bullets. The authorities concerned did question homophobic motives behind the attack. Renato Mendis, a transgender person known otherwise as Thalia, was also murdered brutally in Sao Paolo, Brazil, during 2013. Her body was discovered at home, covered in blood and exhibiting signs of struggle.

In the United States, a transgender woman by the name of Islan Nettles, 21, was attacked in Harlem, New York, in August 2013. She was knocked down by a group of men who beat her up while taunting her with homophobic remarks. Nettles went into a coma after hitting her head on the pavement. She was left brain dead and died within five days.

Islan Nettles

In 2014, Aniya Parker, 47, was targeted in Los Angeles. It appeared to be a robbery which escalated to murder very quickly. Parker was shot in the head in the wee hours of the morning; however, the robbers left her belongings behind. While the police claimed that it was a 'robbery gone bad', LGBT activists insisted that it had all the markings of a hate crime.

Aniya Parker

In Ohio, 2015, a father was responsible for stabbing his own child to death. Transgender Bri Golec, 22, [32] was attacked by Kevin Golec, who later tried to hold the LGBT rights group she supported accountable for the crime. He called the activist group 'a cult' blaming them for Bri's current state. However, the investigating officials found evidence linking him to the murder, and charged him for felony murder and domestic abuse.

Bri Golec

According to several reports, around 20 transgender women were murdered in 2015 during various incidents throughout the USA. Out of these, 18 were African American women.

The Islamic countries are already known for being least tolerant to LGBT community members. People found guilty of engaging in homosexual behavior are handed out severe punishments and sometimes flogged publicly.

Iran created an example out of two boys accused of homosexuality. In 2005, Mahmoud Asgari and Ayaz Marhouni were found guilty of raping a young thirteen-year-old boy. The incident attracted a lot of attention from the international human rights committees, who were of the opinion that the Iranian courts had passed a biased judgment.

It was widely believed that the two youngsters were being punished for homosexuality. They were hanged publicly in Mashhad, Northeast Iran.

Gay and lesbian rights groups did not take this decision well. Members protested that the state of Iran had handed them a death sentence for being homosexuals. Various questions were raised regarding the involvement of the thirteen-year-old boy who was allegedly raped. There were certain groups who differed in their views as well. The verdict was that, whether or not this was a case of homosexuality, further investigation had to be conducted. A number of European countries called out for action and set new protocols for LGBT asylum claimants from Iran.

All this just proves that, despite all the hard work and efforts for LGBT equality, there is still a lot more which is required. It is not just the African, European, Asian or Middle Eastern regions where LGBT community members need to be accepted as equals; the Western countries need to work on it just as much. While many factions of Western societies may be tolerant and peaceful, the homophobic tendencies remain rooted within the system. This is why the number of gender-based hate crimes only seem to increase with time instead of decreasing.

The Orlando Massacre

Gunshots Ruin the Night

Sunday, June 12, 2016, was a fateful day for the 320 people who were enjoying a "Latin Flavor" event at Pulse. Pulse is a gay nightclub in Orlando, Florida. It was around 2 a.m. when an armed gunman killed 50 civilians wounding 53 others.

Omar Mateen, [33] identified as the shooter, lived in Fort Pierce which is 120 miles away from Orlando's gay night club. After Mateen opened fire on the 320 people in the club, a uniformed officer on duty engaged him in a shootout near the club entrance until backup arrived. Additional police officers arrived on the scene and began shooting at the gunman. He then stopped shooting and retreated back to the bathroom where he had held several hostages.

The terrorist made three calls to 911 while he was in the club's bathroom with hostages after he had conducted his initial attack. Mateen remained calm as he communicated with law enforcement about his further carnage. He also mentioned the Boston Marathon bombers and referred to them as "homeboys."

According to FBI director James Comey, the gunman made his first call to 911 after an hour of opening fire, and then hung up. He then called again and talked briefly to the dispatcher and hung up again. The dispatcher called him back. This is when he said that he was doing it for the ISIS leader whom he named and pledged his loyalty to.

The gunman also pledged allegiance to the Islamic state during a call with police negotiators, according to Police Chief John Mina. The Chief added that the gunman was cool and calm during the call; he wasn't asking much, the police negotiator was asking most of the questions.

The authorities attempted to negotiate with the killer, but as the negotiations unraveled and with hostages trapped in the bathroom for hours, the decision was made to breach the wall. The authorities first used an explosive, but it was not effective, so instead they used an armored vehicle to pierce the wall of the club and managed to make an entry hole.

After opening the wall, dozens of hostages were able to escape. Mateen then emerged and was shot dead by the police.

***

Assistant Special Agent in Charge Ronald Hopper of the FBI in Orlando said that the suspect drew the agency's attention in 2013 when he made an inflammatory comment to his fellow co-workers about having ties to terrorism. At that time Mateen was working as a contract security guard at a local courthouse where he told his fellow co-workers that he had ties with al-Qaida and Hezbollah.

Hopper said that, according to the investigation, Mateen told the agency he made the comment out of anger, for he thought his fellow co-workers were teasing him about being a Muslim. Mateen was investigated twice. The second time was in 2014 when he was linked to a US citizen, Moner Mohammad Abu-Salha, who blew himself up in a suicide attack in Syria. They were concerned that Mateen watched the videos made by radical clerical Anwar al-Awlaki. But later Mateen had gotten married and had a child, so they were no longer concerned.

Mateen had a firearm license since September 2011, according to the public records, and was also licensed to be a security officer. In a statement, G4ss said that Mateen had been an employee since September 10, 2007. Hopper added that Mateen legally bought two weapons, a long gun and a handgun, in the days leading up to the shooting. He also tried to buy body armor, but the store didn't sell Kevlar vests.

Although he pledged his allegiance to the Islamic State and shouted Allahu Akbar during the 911 call, his father, Meddique Mir Mateen, claimed that his son's actions had nothing to do with religion, but that a month ago Mateen was angered when he saw two men kissing.

Mourning of Orlando Victims

US President Barrack Obama ordered that the flag of the United States should be flown at half-staff at the White House and upon all public buildings and throughout the United States until the sunset on June 16, 2016, in honor of those who died during the attack.

Hundreds gathered on Boston Common on June 12 for a rally in solidarity with the victims of Orlando shooting.

The vigil was held in Orlando and in different parts of the country to mourn the victims of the attack. Also, a memorial formed at Dr. Phillips Center on June 13, 2016.

The Grand Place, Eiffel Tower and the City Hall of Brussels were illuminated in rainbow colors on June 12 to mourn the victims of the nightclub shooting.

Advocacy and Future Legislative Action

It has already been established that hate crimes against LGBT members are under-reported. This is mainly due to lack of awareness, education and proper protocol in place. Since most of these crimes involve sexual violence, victims are hesitant to report them to the authorities. Many times, even the police do not show interest in pursuing hate crimes or even identifying them as such.

The situation has to be remedied immediately. As violent crimes against gays, lesbians, bisexuals and transgender people increase every year, there is an urgency to bring in a new system which would make it possible for the authorities to pursue such hate crimes in accordance with the law.

Many countries working on establishing legislation on gender-based hate crimes have moved to fast track their resolutions and see to it that appropriate preventive measures are taken.

It has been suggested that law enforcement agencies across the world should train their officers and responders on the ways of classifying a hate crime and handling it properly. These agencies also have a major role to play in creating awareness regarding LGBT hate crimes. The subject requires extensive research which needs to be conducted on various communities, especially the LGBT youth.

Experts have stated that the gay, lesbian and bisexual youngsters are usually prime targets for LGBT hate crimes. In fact, the most common places where rape and forced sexual acts are carried out against these people are school grounds, clubs or popular hangouts.

Hate crimes have affected the lives of people all across the globe. Definitive action is required if the violence against LGBT members is to be curbed. In the United States, the first and foremost step which needs to be taken to ensure peace and co-existence is the smooth enforcement of the Matthew Shepard Hate Crimes Prevention Act. Other than that, societies should play their individual role in helping and supporting each other.

It has been discussed that help centers and counseling, especially catering to LGBT persons, could go a long way in helping the youth in schools and various educational institutions.

A proper LGBT hate crime system is required where the authorities concerned would have to carefully define a gender-bias crime and take action against it. Police officers need to report on such a crime, considering every possible angle and taking into account all the details leading up to the incident.

The advocates of the cause are doing the best they can to bring the plight of LGBT community members in front of everyone. They have tried to highlight the discriminatory behavior that gays, lesbians, bisexuals and transgender people are subjected to in their everyday lives on the basis of their sexual orientation. While change will come with time, one can only hope for a better and brighter future which will be devoid of discrimination and homophobia.

Thank you to my editor, proofreaders, and cover artist for your support:

~ **RJ**

Aeternum Designs (book cover)

Bettye McKee (editor)

Lee Knieper Husemann

Lorrie Suzanne Phillippe

Marlene Fabregas

Darlene Horn

Ron Steed

Katherine McCarthy

Robyn MacEachern

Kathi Garcia

Linda H. Bergeron

About the Author

RJ Parker, Ph.D. is an award-winning and bestselling true crime author and owner of RJ Parker Publishing, Inc. He has written over 20 true crime books which are available in eBook, paperback and audiobook editions, and have sold in over 100 countries. He holds certifications in

Serial Crime, Criminal Profiling and a PhD in Criminology.

To date, RJ has donated over 3,000 autographed books to allied troops serving overseas and to our wounded warriors recovering in Naval and Army hospitals all over the world. He also donates to Victims of Violent Crimes Canada.

If you are a police officer, firefighter, paramedic or serve in the military, active or retired, RJ gives his eBooks freely in appreciation for your service.

Contact Information

Author's Email:

AuthorRJParker@gmail.com

Publisher's Email:

Agent@RJParkerPublishing.com

Website:

http://m.RJPARKERPUBLISHING.com/

Twitter:

http://www.Twitter.com/realRJParker

Facebook:

https://www.Facebook.com/AuthorRJParker

Amazon Author's Page:

rjpp.ca/RJ-PARKER-BOOKS

** SIGN UP FOR OUR MONTLY NEWSLETTER **

http://rjpp.ca/RJ-PARKER-NEWSLETTER

1 https://www.fbi.gov/about-us/cjis/ucr/hate-crime/2012/resource-pages/hate-crime-statistics-act/hatecrimestatisticsact_final

2 https://www.congress.gov/bill/101st-congress/house-bill/1048

3 http://www.conservapedia.com/History_of_homosexuality

4 http://www.historylearningsite.co.uk/nazi-germany/homosexuals-and-nazi-germany/

5 http://www.newworldencyclopedia.org/entry/Gay_rights_movement

6 http://www.revolvy.com/main/index.php?s=Socialism%20and%20LGBT%20rights&item_type=topic

7 http://www.newworldencyclopedia.org/entry/Havelock_Ellis

8 https://newrepublic.com/article/117170/lgbt-rights-sidelined-after-ukrainian-revolution

9 http://rmc.library.cornell.edu/HRC/exhibition/stage/stage_3.html

10 http://thelonglgbtrightsmovement.weebly.com/index.html

11 http://www.civilrights.org/archives/2009/06/449-stonewall.html?referrer=https://www.google.ca/

12 http://library.cqpress.com/cqresearcher/document.php?id=cqresrre1993030500

13 http://www.dailykos.com/story/2011/4/26/970357/-

14 http://gayhistory4u.blogspot.ca/2009/08/in-my-opinion-and-for-many-american-gay.html

15 http://www.missedinhistory.com/podcasts/the-comptons-cafeteria-riot/

16 http://thewhistleblowers.info/the-mafia-ny-city-gay-bars/

17 http://www.britannica.com/event/Stonewall-riots

18 http://www.state.gov/j/drl/rls/hrrpt/2010/wha/154496.htm

19 http://www.towleroad.com/2007/03/two_held_in_bru/

20 http://www.amazon.com/co/1496115201

21 Handbook of LGBT Communities, Crime, and Justice

Dana Peterson, Vanessa R. Panfil

Springer Science & Business Media, Dec 4, 2013

22 http://www.civilrights.org/publications/reports/cause_for_concern/p14.html?referrer=https://www.google.ca/

23 http://www.glbtqarchive.com/ssh/marches_washington_S.pdf

24 http://williamsinstitute.law.ucla.edu/wp-content/uploads/Law-Enforcement-Discrim-Report-Nov-2013.pdf

25 http://www.apadivisions.org/division-19/publications/newsletters/military/2012/09/spotlight-history.aspx

26 http://www.cnn.com/2009/POLITICS/10/28/hate.crimes/

27 http://www.cnn.com/2015/06/26/politics/supreme-court-same-sex-marriage-ruling/

28 http://murderpedia.org/male.J/j/jackson-elton-manning.htm

29 https://www.justice.gov/crt/matthew-shepard-and-james-byrd-jr-hate-crimes-prevention-act-2009-0

30 http://www.gaystarnews.com/article/sakia-gunn-news-coverage-and-gay-hate-murder070613/

31 http://www.bbc.com/news/world-africa-23331832

32 http://www.dailymail.co.uk/news/article-2956413/Father-stabbed-death-transgender-daughter-22-calling-911-saying-killed-fellow-cult-members.html

33 http://www.telegraph.co.uk/news/2016/06/12/omar-mateen-everything-we-know-so-far-about-orlando-gunman/